I0814278

ATHLETES AS INFLUENCERS

Name, Image, and Likeness

By Heather Rule

SportsZone

An Imprint of Abdo Publishing
abdobooks.com

abdobooks.com

Published by Abdo Publishing, a division of ABDO, PO Box 398166, Minneapolis, Minnesota 55439.

Printed in the United States of America, North Mankato, Minnesota.
102025
012026

Cover Photo: Justin Casterline/Getty Images Sport/Getty Images
Interior Photos: Jamie Squire/Getty Images Sport/Getty Images, 1, 29, 30; Jeff Dean/Getty Images Sport/Getty Images, 3, 38–39; Elif Ozturk/Anadolu Agency/Getty Images, 4–5; Stephen McCarthy/Sportsfile/Getty Images, 6; Greg Eans/The Messenger-Inquirer/AP Images, 8; Shutterstock Images, 11; Brian Spurlock/Icon Sportswire/Getty Images, 12–13; Jonathan Weiss/Shutterstock Images, 14; Bernstein Associates/Getty Images Sport/Getty Images, 16; Isaac Brekken/AP Images, 17; Joel Auerbach/Getty Images Sport/Getty Images, 19; Bongarts/Getty Images, 21; Aytac Unal/Anadolu/Getty Images, 22–23, 45; Jean Catuffe/Getty Images Sport/Getty Images, 24–25; Amin Mohammad Jamali/Getty Images Sport/Getty Images, 26–27; Reagan Cotton/LSU/University Images/Getty Images, 32–33; Ed Zurga/Getty Images Sport/Getty Images, 34–35; Alika Jenner/Getty Images Sport/Getty Images, 37; Joe Robbins/Icon Sportswire/Getty Images, 41; Michael Owens/Getty Images Sport/Getty Images, 42; Sam Hodde/Getty Images Sport/Getty Images, 43, 47

Editor: Christa Kelly
Series Designer: Maggie Villaume

Library of Congress Control Number: 2025939165

Publisher's Cataloging-in-Publication Data

Names: Rule, Heather, author.
Title: Athletes as influencers: name, image, and likeness / by Heather Rule
Description: Minneapolis, Minnesota: Abdo Publishing, 2026 | Series: The business of sports | Includes online resources and index.
Identifiers: ISBN 9781098298234 (lib. bdg.) | ISBN 9798384932031 (ebook)
Subjects: LCSH: Sports--Juvenile literature. | Athletes--Juvenile literature. | Social media in sports--Juvenile literature. | Social media influencers--Juvenile literature. | Internet personalities--Juvenile literature. | Sports in popular culture--Juvenile literature.
Classification: DDC 070.449796--dc23

TABLE OF CONTENTS

Chapter One

ATHLETE AND ENTREPRENEUR 4

Chapter Two

THE HISTORY OF NIL 12

Chapter Three

OLYMPIC ATHLETES AND NIL 22

Chapter Four

NIL TODAY 34

TIMELINE 44

GLOSSARY 46

MORE INFORMATION 47

ONLINE RESOURCES 47

INDEX 48

ABOUT THE AUTHOR 48

CHAPTER ONE

ATHLETE AND ENTREPRENEUR

In the spring of 2020, the COVID-19 pandemic brought the world to a screeching halt. With the world on pause, Chloe Mitchell was looking for something to do. Mitchell was a high school senior and star volleyball player in Michigan. Stuck in lockdown, she needed something to keep her busy.

"I was bored," Mitchell recalled. "I was quite honestly really depressed because quarantine had taken away my senior year, I had no prom, and you know, we're all down in the dumps because of COVID. I needed something to take my mind off things."

Mitchell decided to spend her free time turning a small shed in her family's backyard into a cozy retreat. She posted videos of her process on TikTok. Followers joined Mitchell as she cleaned

The COVID-19 pandemic closed schools and paused sports for more than a year in some places.

Creators can monetize their TikTok accounts to earn money from their content.

out the shed and transformed it into the perfect hideaway. The final shed had a mini fridge, a daybed, a giant beanbag, hanging plants, and a small table and chair. Strings of lights were wrapped around the ceiling beams, bathing the shed in a warm glow.

To Mitchell's surprise, millions of people tuned in to watch her renovation project. Her videos routinely got hundreds of thousands of views. By December 23, 2020, Mitchell had more than 5,500 followers on YouTube, 48,600 followers on Instagram, and 2.7 million followers on TikTok.

As Mitchell's popularity grew, she started getting sponsorships for her videos. Her first sponsorship was from Smart Cups. The company sold beverages. Smart Cups paid Mitchell $3,000 to advertise their products. The money helped Mitchell pay for a computer she planned to take to college. She also made enough money from her videos to pay for a car outright.

Summer slowly drew to a close. Mitchell began to worry about making videos. She had a partial academic and athletic scholarship to play volleyball for Aquinas College in Grand Rapids, Michigan. Mitchell knew that her influencer career could jeopardize her ability to play college volleyball.

NIL Comes to the NAIA

For most of history, college sports were strictly amateur. That meant athletes were not allowed to be paid for competing in sports. They were also forbidden from profiting off their name, image, and likeness (NIL). This is another way of saying that a well-known college athlete couldn't use their fame to earn money by, for example, partnering with a brand to advertise its products.

Mitchell understood that these rules could be a problem for her. She was accepting sponsorships for her videos. This meant she was profiting from her NIL. She worried that

she'd be forced to give up her passion for either volleyball or content creation.

Luckily for Mitchell, her college's NIL rules changed just in time. Aquinas College is part of the National Association of Intercollegiate Athletics (NAIA). The NAIA is similar to the much larger National Collegiate Athletic Association (NCAA) but regulates sports in smaller colleges. In October 2020, the NAIA passed rules that allowed the association's student-athletes to be paid for the use of their NIL. This meant that Mitchell could continue to monetize her social media. She could also promote products and accept sponsorships.

At the beginning of Mitchell's first college volleyball season, she secured her first sponsorships as a college athlete. She promoted golf products from Bloodline Golf and Delta Putt. This made Mitchell the first college athlete to legally make money from her NIL.

PARTNERING WITH PROFESSIONALS

Chloe Mitchell's dad is Keith Mitchell. He is a tech entrepreneur and former college athlete. In 2020, the pair started PlayBooked. PlayBooked is a networking site that helps college athletes connect with brands. It's one of the many businesses that have stepped in to help athletes profit from their NIL. Opendorse is another such company. It launched in 2012 and helps athletes navigate NIL deals.

A New Era in NIL

The new NAIA rules allowed schools to make guidelines for athletes about how they could

More than 83,000 students play sports in the NAIA each year.

monetize their NIL. Some schools prohibited athletes from wearing their school colors or uniforms in ads. Others allowed athletes to collaborate only with certain brands. Many required student-athletes to report their NIL profits to their athletics department once a year. Mitchell said that her college made this reporting process easy.

Mitchell believes the NAIA's new NIL rules benefited more than just her wallet. She said her sponsorships helped her learn about networking and making contracts. Those are lessons she can take into her postcollegiate career.

Mitchell believes she's proof that changing NIL rules can be beneficial to college athletes, even those competing for smaller schools. Some critics feared the use of NIL would be unfair to less famous athletes, especially women. But Mitchell's story challenges this narrative. She was a volleyball player at a small school who made enough money to pay off her student loans. She didn't have to be one of the most famous athletes in the country to be both a college athlete and an entrepreneur.

Between 2022 and 2023, NIL compensation for college women's volleyball players increased by 365 percent.

JW MARRIOTT
IS IT IN YOU?
IS IT IN YOU?

CHAPTER TWO

THE HISTORY OF NIL

Founded in 1906, the NCAA began as a body to regulate college football. Today it's the main governing body for college sports, with more than 1,000 member schools across its three divisions. For much of the NCAA's history, its rules required athletes to be amateurs.

Initially, many students were banned from even receiving scholarships for playing sports. But even after this changed, the NCAA banned athletes from earning money from competing. They also could not use their NIL to earn money. Students forfeited, or gave up, their NIL rights when they signed on to play a sport with a college team. It wasn't until the 2020s that the rules changed. Athletes were finally allowed to receive money for their NIL. But the battle for college NIL rights stretches back decades.

Brands can use athletes' fame to introduce their products to wider audiences.

The NCAA was founded in 1906. Today, more than 520,000 students play for NCAA teams.

Early NCAA

The NCAA used to be very strict about forbidding student-athletes from receiving compensation for playing college sports. It stressed that student-athletes were amateurs and therefore couldn't profit from playing sports. The people in charge of college sports believed athletes should be playing for the love of the game and for their schools. Earning money as a college athlete was seen as against the spirit of college athletics.

Many athletes did not think this was fair. After all, the schools were making money off their sports teams. They could charge large sums to broadcast games and sell merchandise. Over time, people began challenging the NCAA's rules.

In 1956, the NCAA changed its rules to allow schools to give students athletic scholarships. But its rules were strict about what the scholarships could cover. The organization ruled that the scholarships could cover only tuition, room, food, books, and some incidental expenses such as laundry. By 1976, covering incidental expenses was banned again.

Challenging the System

Though the NCAA allowed students to accept scholarships in exchange for their athletic talent, many student-athletes wanted more. They wanted to be able to profit from their NIL. In some cases, an athlete's NIL could be very valuable. For example, the star quarterback at a big school might be able to earn millions off their NIL. But even athletes from smaller sports could benefit.

One of the first defining moments in the fight over NIL rules happened in 2009. The video game company Electronic Arts (EA) had released a new game called

NCAA March Madness. The athletes in the game were based on real college basketball players. EA paid the NCAA for the right to make the game. But EA didn't pay the athletes. It couldn't under NCAA rules. Even retired players could not earn money from their college athletic careers.

Many players didn't think this was fair. Ed O'Bannon was one of them. O'Bannon was a former University of California, Los Angeles (UCLA), basketball player. EA had used his likeness and jersey number in the game. The company had also used the

In 1995, Ed O'Bannon helped UCLA win the NCAA men's basketball championship.

In 2018, O'Bannon published a book about his experience suing the NCAA.

jersey numbers and likenesses of his friends. None of them had been paid.

"Most of my teammates never earned a dime," O'Bannon said, "but there they were in this video game, selling for $60, while the NCAA gets paid." O'Bannon sued EA and the NCAA. But he didn't sue for money. He sued to force the NCAA to change its NIL rules. "Not everything's about money or fame," O'Bannon said. "This is about basic fairness and dignity."

EA didn't want the case to go to trial. The company settled. This means that the company agreed to pay O'Bannon and the other players in exchange for the players dropping the lawsuit. EA paid $40 million to O'Bannon and the other athletes.

The NCAA did not want to settle. The case went to trial, and O'Bannon won. The NCAA was ordered to change its rules. This proved to be the first step in allowing athletes to earn money off their NIL.

When judges make decisions about cases, they will often reference other past decisions. Many judges have cited O'Bannon's case in expanding NIL rules. O'Bannon is happy that he's made a difference. He said, "It feels good to see justice arrive. It's been a long battle."

NCAA v. Alston

The NCAA went back to court in 2014. A group of NCAA athletes sued the organization. The athletes did not think it was fair that the NCAA could forbid them from being compensated for playing sports. Their lawsuit was called *NCAA v. Alston*.

The case first went to the court of the Northern District of California. The court agreed with the athletes. It ordered the NCAA to change its strict rules regarding student-athlete compensation. The NCAA appealed the findings. The case took a long time to resolve. The matter eventually went to

One of the main athletes suing the NCAA in *NCAA v. Alston* was former West Virginia running back Shawne Alston.

the US Supreme Court in 2021. The Supreme Court agreed with the lower courts and dismissed the appeal. One justice said, "Nowhere else in America can businesses get away with agreeing not to pay their workers a fair market rate on the theory that their product is defined by not paying their workers a fair market rate. . . . The NCAA is not above the law."

The NCAA finally decided to allow students to profit from their NIL. Student-athletes were free to partner with brands. They could profit from social media. They could finally monetize their fame.

Professional Athletes

NIL deals aren't just for college athletes. Professional athletes make money from their NIL too. Some make money by advertising products. Others make their own products.

In 1905, Louisville Slugger wanted more people to know about its baseball bats. Pittsburgh Pirates shortstop Honus Wagner was one of the sport's biggest stars at the time. So Louisville Slugger paid him to put his autograph on the bat. It's considered to be the first athlete endorsement of a sports product.

Professional athletes have been making money off their NIL ever since. Perhaps no athlete has been as successful at it as Michael Jordan. Jordan signed a contract with Nike in 1984 as a National Basketball Association (NBA) rookie. This was unusual at the time. Most brands signed deals with entire teams. But Nike wanted to try something new.

Jordan's contract with Nike was worth $2.5 million over five years. Under the contract, Nike would design a shoe and use Jordan's name and likeness to promote it.

EARNING WITH NIL

Athletes can use their NIL to make money in many different ways. Some are paid to wear certain brands. Others are paid to promote certain brands on social media. Still others appear in ad campaigns. Some players partner with brands to create new products. Athletes may also be paid for making appearances or giving speeches.

In addition to Nike, Michael Jordan partnered with other brands such as Gatorade and Hanes.

The deal ended up being a game changer for Jordan, Nike, and the world of sports.

Nike designed a new pair of shoes. The shoes came to be known as the Jordan 1. The shoes were black and red. They matched the Bulls' colors. The shoes were released on April 1, 1985. Nike sold them for $65 a pair.

With Jordan's name attached to the brand, the shoes' popularity exploded. Nike made more than $100 million from the shoes by the end of that year. After the success of Jordan's partnership with Nike, other brands began to make NIL deals with individual athletes. Jordan's deal led the way for more athletes to make money from sponsorships.

CHAPTER THREE

OLYMPIC ATHLETES AND NIL

The modern Olympic Games began in 1896 as a multi-sport competition for amateurs. Similar to college sports, the athletes couldn't be paid for their performances or accept NIL deals. These restrictions started to change in the 1970s. By the 1980s, many events in the Olympic Games were opened to professional athletes as well as amateurs.

It isn't cheap to be an Olympian. For many, being an athlete is a full-time job. Athletes train year-round, including in non-Olympic years. They often have to travel to other countries to compete. Paying for coaches and equipment can be expensive too. National teams often help cover these costs. Sometimes they pay athletes

Many Olympic athletes are well known. Brands partner with them to capitalize on the athletes' fame.

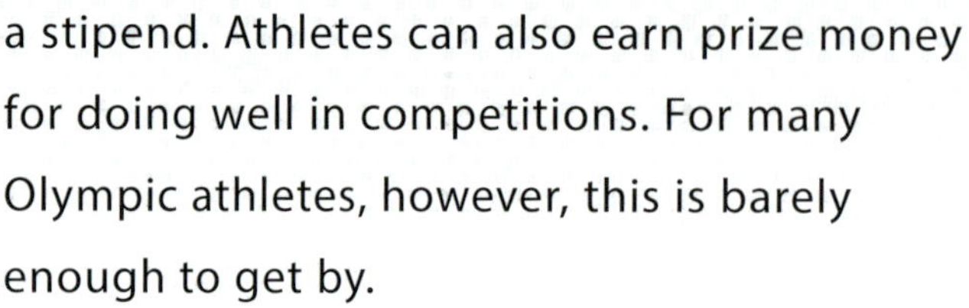

a stipend. Athletes can also earn prize money for doing well in competitions. For many Olympic athletes, however, this is barely enough to get by.

NIL deals can be lifelines for Olympic athletes. They allow athletes to earn money through endorsements, sponsorships, and social media partnerships. Many Olympians capitalize on their NIL.

Simone Biles is the most decorated gymnast of all time. But she earns about 99 percent of her income away from the gym through NIL deals. She has partnered with companies such as GK Elite, Nike, and Athleta. As part of her partnerships with these brands, she wears the brands' clothes at competitions.

During the 2024 Paris Olympics, Simone Biles brought her Olympic medal count up to 11.

PARIS 2024

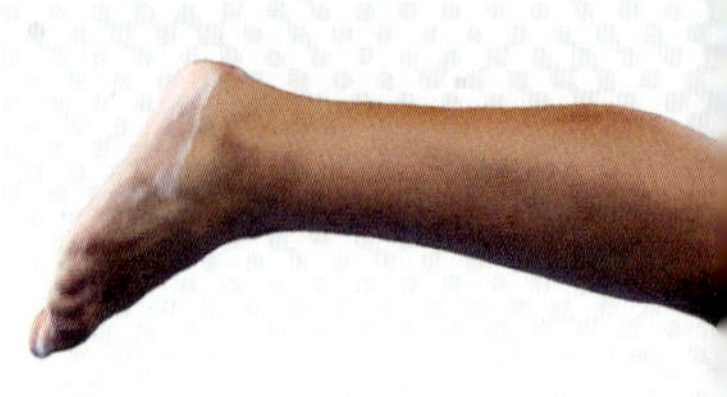

She even partnered with Athleta to make her own exercise clothing line for teens. Biles has also partnered with several nonclothing brands. These brands include Visa, Uber Eats, and K18. These partnerships bring in millions of dollars for Biles.

Student Olympians

Even after Olympic athletes became eligible for NIL deals, the rules remained tricky for athletes who wanted to compete on both the Olympic and college levels. Many elite gymnasts faced a difficult choice during their teenage years. They could compete professionally and try to earn as much money as possible. Or they could remain amateurs. Both could qualify for the Olympics. But only amateur gymnasts could also compete in college. Gymnasts had to determine if a potential college scholarship would be more valuable than the money they'd earn from NIL deals.

In the 2020s, the NCAA rules changed. Elite gymnasts no longer had to decide between professional and college gymnastics. This opened doors for gymnasts. It also allowed them to change their minds about their career paths.

The 2024 US Olympic gymnastics team is a great example of how the change in NIL rules benefited athletes. Suni Lee,

Jordan Chiles earned a silver medal at the Tokyo Olympics in 2021.

Jordan Chiles, and Jade Carey were part of the US gymnastics team at the 2021 Olympics in Tokyo, Japan. Upon returning home, each began an NCAA gymnastics career. This benefited the athletes more than just financially. The ability to compete in the NCAA for their schools helped the athletes stay in shape and compete more frequently than they would have if they'd competed only in professional gymnastics.

After winning the Olympic all-around gold medal, Lee started college at Auburn University. Her high-profile win afforded her a lot of NIL opportunities. Because of the new NCAA rules, she was able to take advantage of those opportunities while also competing for her school.

Meanwhile, Carey began establishing herself as a star at Oregon State. Chiles competed for UCLA. All three enjoyed success at the college level. Lee and Chiles became NCAA champions. Carey also reached the podium in multiple NCAA Championships. Along the way, all three continued to build their followings and earn money through NIL deals.

When the next Olympics rolled around in 2024, Lee, Carey, and Chiles decided to go for another shot at the Games. Such a decision would have been unheard of just a few years earlier. College gymnastics is a lower level than the Olympics, so gymnasts traditionally only entered the college arena when their elite careers were over. But with the help of new NIL rules, the three gymnasts were able to succeed on both levels.

Ultimately, all three ended up making the 2024 Olympics in Paris, France. Lee earned bronze medals in the all-around and the uneven bars. Carey won a bronze medal on vault. Meanwhile, all three contributed to the winning team score. Lee had left Auburn by then. But Carey and Chiles became the first gymnasts to win Olympic gold medals in the middle of their NCAA careers.

"That's the best thing about NIL," said Vanessa Atler, one of the top US gymnasts during the late 1990s.

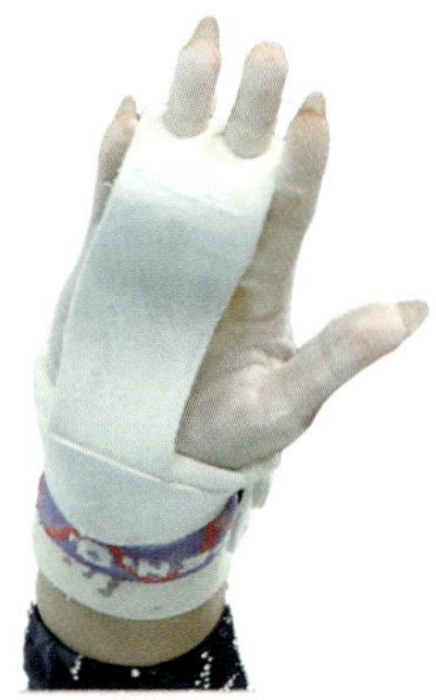

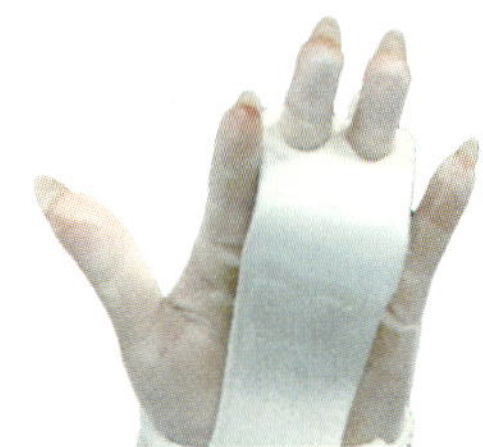

During the Tokyo Olympics and the 2024 Paris Olympics, Suni Lee won six medals.

PARIS 2024
PARIS 2024

"It's giving the power back to the athletes."

Social Media

Just as NIL deals can help support Olympic athletes, the Olympics can help athletes secure NIL deals. The Olympics are extremely popular. Televised events introduce athletes to audiences. Many people follow their favorite athletes on social media. As an athlete's social media following increases, so does the amount of money the athlete can charge for NIL deals. The athlete becomes more valuable because their promotions will reach more people.

AGENTS

Many professional athletes hire agents to help them manage their NIL deals. Agents advise athletes on which companies to work with. They also help their clients find new NIL opportunities. In return, they often get a percentage of what the athlete makes. For example, Simone Biles relies on her agent Janey Miller to help her navigate NIL deals. Miller works for a bigger company called Octagon that represents athletes. Some athletes also hire other professionals to help them with marketing, legal issues, and other business matters.

The popularity of the 2024 US gymnastics team perfectly illustrates this concept. After the 2024 Olympics, Carey gained 185,063 new followers on Instagram. This was a 56.7 percent increase. This increase in followers increased the amount of money she could make from NIL deals. Before the Olympics, Carey's rate for a branded social media post in partnership

Jade Carey won the bronze medal on the vault during the 2024 Paris Olympics.

with large companies was between $3,500 and $4,900 per post. After the 2024 Olympics, that amount increased to $8,500 to $11,600 per post. Carey has capitalized on her success by signing NIL deals with Reebok, Amazon, Cracker Jack, and more.

Chiles saw a jump in followers after the Olympics too. Before the 2024 Olympics, Chiles had 571,244 followers on Instagram. That number jumped to 991,943 after the Olympics. This is a 79.7 percent increase. Chiles's fame has helped her secure brand deals with businesses such as Nike and Toyota. She also launched an athletic wear business called Melanin Drip Clothing Company.

Lee's follower count also jumped after the Games. She went from about 1.6 million Instagram followers to roughly 2.4 million followers. Lee used this fame and her Olympic success to seize brand deals with Crocs, Amazon, and Target. Lee, like many athletes, is reaping the benefits of the NCAA's new NIL rules.

CASE STUDY

LIVVY DUNNE

Gymnast Livvy Dunne started building her social media following at age 10. She documented her journey in and out of the gym. Over the years, she grew her audience to millions of followers on Instagram and TikTok.

Dunne's audience followed her to Louisiana State University (LSU) in the fall of 2020. As a result, Dunne was positioned to benefit when the NCAA loosened its NIL rules soon after. Dunne was at the center of NIL from the start. She was featured on a billboard in Times Square sponsored by LSU. The TikTok she posted with the billboard was viewed nearly 20 million times. Other NIL deals came streaming in. Dunne partnered with businesses such as Nautica, American Eagle, Vuori, and Bodyarmor. By 2025, Dunne's NIL endorsement deals were estimated at $4.1 million. This meant that Dunne was making more from NIL deals than any other female college athlete in the country.

It took practice for Dunne to learn to balance her personal life with her athletic, school, and influencer careers. But Dunne learned to manage her many roles. She now runs the Livvy Fund. This organization helps connect LSU's female athletes with NIL opportunities.

Livvy Dunne hired the talent agency William Morris Endeavor to negotiate her NIL deals.

COLORA
2

CHAPTER FOUR

NIL TODAY

Today, NIL deals are great ways for both professional athletes and college athletes to earn money. With the new rule changes, college athletes are quickly stepping up to capitalize on their NIL. Many are striking massive deals.

Former University of Colorado quarterback Shedeur Sanders is proof of how far college athletes have come with NIL deals. In 2024, Sanders became one of college football's top earners with an estimated $6.2 million in NIL deals. With that amount of money, he was earning more from NIL deals than some professional football players earn through their salaries. He became the first college football player to sign with Nike.

Top basketball recruit Paige Bueckers has made use of her NIL too. Bueckers arrived at Connecticut in 2020, just as NIL opportunities were opening up to NCAA athletes. She racked up multiple NIL deals in 2021. Bueckers was the first collegiate athlete

Shedeur Sanders played for Jackson State University from 2021 to 2022 and the University of Colorado Boulder from 2023 to 2024.

to sign a deal with Gatorade. She also signed a deal with Nike.

NIL COLLECTIVES

With the NCAA now allowing students to profit from their NIL, college boosters are looking for ways to compensate their schools' athletes. One way they are doing this is through NIL collectives. NIL collectives are organizations that support student-athletes from specific colleges. These collectives pool money from donors. They then distribute the money to athletes in exchange for the athletes appearing at events or promoting certain brands.

Caitlin Clark

Endorsements and NIL deals are especially important for female professional athletes. Female athletes are generally paid much less than male athletes. NIL deals can help bridge this gap. They can bring in more money for athletes than the athletes' salaries. Though men have more NIL opportunities than women, female athletes have still found success with NIL deals.

Basketball player Caitlin Clark has used her NIL to bring in big deals. Clark had a historic college career playing basketball at the University of Iowa from 2020 to 2024. She averaged 31.6 points per game. She became college basketball's all-time leading scorer. Clark also led Iowa to two national championship games.

Clark was the top overall pick for the Women's National Basketball Association (WNBA) in 2024 and signed with the

Caitlin Clark's No. 22 jersey was retired after her career at the University of Iowa.

IOWA
22
Wilson

Indiana Fever. Her contract and bonus with the WNBA totaled about $100,000 for one year. But her total earnings for the year were $11.1 million. Clark made most of her money through endorsement deals. She has NIL deals with Gatorade, State Farm, Wilson, Hy-Vee, Xfinity, Gainbridge, Lilly, and the trading card company Panini America.

One of Clark's biggest partnerships is with Nike. In April 2024, Nike signed Clark to an eight-year deal worth more than $3 million per year. It's one of the biggest endorsement deals in women's basketball history.

Creative Deals

Brands don't always choose the most popular or most successful athletes

Clark signed a deal with Wilson Sporting Goods Co. to produce a signature collection of basketballs.

for partnerships. Some brands partner with athletes for more creative reasons. Decoldest Crawford was a wide receiver for the University of Nebraska. In 2022, Crawford signed a deal with an Omaha-based heating and cooling company. He appeared in a commercial for the company and said, "I'm always Decoldest." He turned his name into a marketing tool. The ad went viral.

Another college football player also used his name to secure a brand deal. Bijan Robinson was one of the best running backs in the nation. He played for the University of Texas from 2020 to 2022. During his three seasons at the college, he had 3,410 rushing yards and made 41 touchdowns. In 2022, Robinson started using both his fame and his name to make NIL deals. He launched a line of Dijon mustard called Bijan Mustardson, a play on the athlete's name. The slogan on the mustard bottle read, "It's like a touchdown in your mouth." Robinson also made NIL deals with Lamborghini and Raising Canes.

Ga'Quincy McKinstry was a cornerback for the University of Alabama. From his birth, family members called McKinstry by his nickname, Kool-Aid. In 2021, McKinstry signed an NIL deal with the Kool-Aid drink company.

Dieunerst Collin went viral at nine years old. One day, someone took a video of Collin holding a Popeyes drink cup and staring suspiciously at the camera. A still from that video turned into a meme. Nearly a decade later, Collin began playing as a center for Lake Erie College in Ohio. SportsCenter shared a photo of Collin after his high school state championship next to the Popeyes meme. Collin shared the post and tagged Popeyes. Before long, Popeyes signed an NIL deal with Collin.

Giving Back

Athletes use the money they receive from their NIL deals in different ways. Many use the money to pay for their educational expenses. But some student-athletes use their NIL profits to give back to their communities.

In 2025, Texas quarterback Arch Manning made more money with his NIL deals than any other college or high school athlete. Arch's uncles are former professional football stars Peyton and Eli Manning. This means that Arch was well known even before his college football debut. He quickly began bringing in NIL deals.

Arch used some of the profits from his NIL deals to help others. One of his NIL deals was with Panini America. The company auctioned off a trading card of Arch with plans to give the athlete the money to donate to a good cause. The card sold for $102,500. Arch donated the money to the Ronald McDonald House Charities.

In 2025, Arch Manning's NIL deals were estimated at $6.6 million.

HORNS
PEACH
BOWL
TEXAS

In 2022, Tyler Linderbaum was selected to play for the Baltimore Ravens.

University of Iowa offensive lineman Tyler Linderbaum donated his earnings as well. Linderbaum made a donation of $30,000 to charity. This was Linderbaum's entire earnings over six months. The money went to the University of Iowa Stead Family Children's Hospital. This hospital is near the team's stadium. Iowa football players, fans, and coaches wave to the kids watching games from their hospital windows.

NIL deals have long been an important source of income for professional athletes. Today, these deals are becoming important for college athletes too. Though many opposed the NCAA's and NAIA's rule changes, athletes are seeing massive benefits from the changes and are learning important business lessons in the process.

CASE STUDY

ROCCO BECHT

Rocco Becht is the son of former National Football League (NFL) player Anthony Becht. Anthony Becht used to host football camps for aspiring players. Today, Rocco is carrying on his father's tradition.

Rocco Becht went from a backup quarterback to the face of the Iowa State football program. As a freshman in 2023, he threw for 3,120 yards and 23 touchdowns. He also ran for 63 yards and three touchdowns.

Rocco's performance and social media presence helped him land several NIL partnerships with local businesses. He also partnered with EA Sports to be featured in the highly anticipated *College Football 25* video game. Rocco donated $7,500 of the money he made from NIL deals. The money went to a local youth football program. Rocco also hosted a free football camp for kids in July 2024. Several of his Iowa State teammates helped him coach the camp. About 100 kids in grades five through eight participated. Rocco hoped to continue to give his time and NIL money to support communities in need.

In 2025, Rocco Becht donated some of his NIL earnings to a local children's hospital.

TIMELINE

1906

On March 31, the NCAA forms to regulate college football.

1956

The NCAA changes its rules to allow student-athletes to receive athletic scholarships. However, these scholarships are limited to paying for tuition, rooms, food, books, and incidentals.

1976

The NCAA updates its rules to forbid scholarships from paying for incidental expenses.

1980s

Olympic events are open to professional athletes in addition to amateur athletes.

1984

On October 26, NBA rookie Michael Jordan signs a contract with Nike.

2009

On July 21, Ed O'Bannon, a former basketball player at UCLA, sues EA and the NCAA after his likeness is used in an EA video game without compensation.

2014

A group of NCAA athletes sues the organization for banning athletes from receiving compensation for playing sports. The case goes to court in *NCAA v. Alston*.

2020

On October 6, the NAIA passes rules allowing NIL compensation for student-athletes. Aquinas College volleyball player Chloe Mitchell is the first college athlete to legally make money from her NIL.

2021

On June 21, the US Supreme Court rejects the NCAA's appeal of *NCAA v. Alston*. The NCAA changes its rules to allow student-athletes to benefit financially from their NIL.

2024

On August 28, University of Colorado quarterback Shedeur Sanders becomes the first college football player to sign a deal with Nike.

GLOSSARY

amateur

A person who plays a sport without getting paid.

appeal

A legal proceeding submitted to ask a higher court to review the decision of a lower court.

capitalize

To take advantage of an opportunity.

compensate

To give someone money in exchange for work.

elite

The highest level.

endorsement

A deal in which an athlete promotes a company in exchange for the company's products or money.

incidental

Minor and connected to a larger thing.

monetize

To use something to make money.

pandemic

A widespread outbreak of a disease that affects a large portion of the population.

professional

A person who gets paid to perform.

rookie

A professional athlete in their first year of competition.

scholarship

Money awarded to a student to pay for education expenses.

stipend

Money paid to cover expenses.

student-athlete

A student who participates in an organized sport sponsored by their institution.

MORE INFORMATION

BOOKS

Beattie, Charlie. *Sports Brands: The Companies at the Center of the Action.* Abdo, 2026.

McDougall, Chrös. *GOATs of College Football*. Abdo, 2026.

The Story of the Olympic Games. Welbeck, 2021.

ONLINE RESOURCES

To learn more about name, image, and likeness, please visit **abdobooklinks.com** or scan this QR code. These links are routinely monitored and updated to provide the most current information available.

INDEX

Atler, Vanessa, 29

Becht, Rocco, 43
Biles, Simone, 24–26, 31
Bueckers, Paige, 35–36

Carey, Jade, 27–29, 31–32
Chiles, Jordan, 27–29, 32
Clark, Caitlin, 36–38
college athletes, 5–10, 13–20, 26–29, 32, 33, 35–36, 39–42, 43
Collin, Dieunerst, 39–40
Crawford, Decoldest, 39

Dunne, Livvy, 33

Jordan, Michael, 20–21

Lee, Suni, 26–29, 32
Linderbaum, Tyler, 42

Manning, Arch, 40
McKinstry, Ga'Quincy, 39
Mitchell, Chloe, 5–9, 10

National Association of Intercollegiate Athletics (NAIA), 9–10, 42
National Basketball Association (NBA), 20
National Collegiate Athletic Association (NCAA), 9, 13–19, 26–29, 33, 35, 36, 42
National Football League (NFL), 43
NCAA v. Alston, 18–19

O'Bannon, Ed, 16–18
Olympic Games, 23–32

professional athletes, 20–21, 23–32, 35, 36–38, 40, 42, 43

Robinson, Bijan, 39

Sanders, Shedeur, 35
social media, 5–9, 19, 20, 24, 31–32, 33, 40, 43

Wagner, Honus, 20
Women's National Basketball Association (WNBA), 36–37

ABOUT THE AUTHOR

Heather Rule is a writer and sports journalist. She has a bachelor's degree in journalism and mass communication from the University of St. Thomas.